Siddhartha's Existential Crisis/ The Buddha's Resolution

"He, who injures living beings, is not Noble. He is called Noble, because he is gentle and kind towards all living beings." Buddha.

"In the past, monks, and also now, I teach Dukkha and the cessation of Dukkha." Buddha

Introduction

This book examines relevant factors, as different from the Traditional texts' stories, regarding Siddhartha Gautama's psychological crisis causing him to leave his home and renounce the secular life at age 29. A primary assertion of this paper is that the traditional story of the 'Four Sights' is allegorical and the description of Siddhartha's psychological and emotional response to them is better understood what modern psychology calls an existential crisis or crisis in understanding life. An apparent significant factor in his renunciation is that Siddhartha Gautama and his family were members of the Kshatriya or warrior/leader caste, and it is a fact which is usually not elaborated on in many Traditional texts.

Dukkha, or often translated as suffering, was the key element of Siddhartha's crisis and is the focus of all Buddhist doctrine in the Four Noble Truths. The Buddha put suffering as the focus of his inquiry and he taught the doctrine of The Four Noble Truths; the truth of suffering (Dukkha), the truth of the origin of suffering (Samudāya), the truth of the cessation of suffering (Nirodha), and the truth of the Path to the cessation of suffering (Magga). However, in Buddhist thought there is a wide discussion about the meaning of suffering. In this book a definition of Dukkha with its variations will be provided.Siddhartha's response to suffering became the impetus for him to seek a life of renunciation to answer his perplexity about Dukkha and its cessation.

Finally, Gautama Siddhartha's original crisis, told in the symbolic story of the Four Sights, strongly brought the problem of Dukkha to the forefront of his awareness. This is the significance of the legend from the Four Sights. Their lesson is that besides ordinary physical and emotional pain, there is a deeper existential grief and discontent resulting from one's awareness of life's inherent impermanence and groundlessness. Awakening or Enlightenment became the basis of the resolution of his personal crisis leading to the formulation of the Four Noble Truths.

Since most people try to understand the Buddha's teachings from the common perspective based on duality, substantialism and egotism, suffering is understood as physical or emotional pain- unhappiness in the sensual, material, egotistical sense of aversion and disappointments in life. In the past, when this perspective was used, the Buddha's teachings were interpreted as a pessimistic theory due to the impossibility that one can always have or keep what he/she wants; therefore, the interpretation was 'Life is Suffering'. Nonetheless, this is not the teaching of the Buddha.

This paper advocates that instead the Buddha found a solution to existential sorrow and alienation and the greed and hatred created through being ignorant of the true nature of life.

Siddhartha Gautama's Life

There is clear agreement that there was a historical man named Siddhartha Gautama, who became The Buddha and taught the Noble Eightfold Path. Also, the original experience of the Buddha's Awakening, has been repeatedly validated after two thousand years by the successful use of the Eightfold Path as a spiritually transformative vehicle that leads to Awakening. However, what is known about his life can only be sketched from the traditional texts, many of them appear allegorical, and the historical context.

Scholars tend to agree that the editors of the final versions of Buddha's many biographies made their own additions and shaped the contents of the texts according to their own interests, and to support their philosophical and religious ideas. Nevertheless, both modern scholars and the Buddhist tradition agree that the Buddha lived for 80 years. Also, it is commonly agreed that Siddhartha belonged to the Sahkya clan who lived mainly located at the foot of the Himalayas, and he was born in the Gautama family. Because of this, in the Mahayana literature, he became known as Shakyamuni or 'sage of the Shakya clan'. His father's name was Suddhodana and his mother's name was Maya. Siddhartha's family lived in a city named Kapilavastu, and it is believed that Siddhartha was born in Lumbini, present day Nepal, not far from Kapilavastu.

The traditional story says that when Prince Siddhartha was a few days old, a holy man or by some accounts, nine Brahman holy men, made a prophecy about him. It was foretold that the boy would be either a great ruler or a great spiritual teacher. King Suddhodana preferred the first outcome and raised his son accordingly. Apparently, Siddhartha's family was a leading family within the clan's political system and his father was a clan chief. Siddhartha and his family were members of the Kshatriya or warrior/leader caste.

The Kshatriya Culture

To better understand Siddhartha and later the Buddha, it is important to know the probable significant effects of his caste, the Kshatriya, on his personality development and identity. In fact, modern research indicates that caste identity and relying on caste norms, often provide feelings of belongingness or self-esteem. Particularly, it is known that high caste individuals, as the kshatriya were, see caste identity as a stable construct since this identity is inherited at birth. They tend to characterize their identity as intrinsic and this is predominantly attributed to the feelings of connectedness with previous generations of one's caste group. High caste individuals also develop feelings of temporal continuity, positive distinctiveness, and heightened selfesteem from the intrinsic nature of their caste identity.[1]

The Kshatriya Caste

"And now I, the venerable and fully enlightened one, was born a warrior and have come from the caste of warriors, o monks." Buddha

At the time of Siddhartha, there were four Varna, social orders or castes of society. The four classes were: brahmin, kshatriya, vaishya and shudra. The texts show that Siddhartha's caste was the Kshatriya caste (the warrior-rulers caste). The term kshatriya means 'noble warrior' and like all kshatriya men, Siddhartha would have trained from a very young age to be a warrior. Also, according to the Indo-Aryan rule of primogeniture or the exclusive right of inheritance or preference to the eldest male child above all others, Siddhartha, as his father/chief's eldest son, was expected to succeed his father as chief of the clan.

The traditional texts are clear that Siddhartha and his family were members of the Kshatriya caste. The fundamental duty of a Kshatriya was to protect their territory, defend against attacks, deliver justice, govern virtuously, and extend peace and happiness to all their subjects, a 'defender of the poor', and they would counsel in matters of territorial sovereignty and ethical dilemmas. In addition, the Kshatriya caste also played a very important role in the development of Indian political thought and are thought to have authored key early texts of political strategy such as the Arthashastra or treatise on rulership, economic policy and military strategy. The Arthashastra was composed, expanded and redacted between the 2nd century BCE and 3rd century CE, and was influential until the 12th century, when it disappeared. It was rediscovered in 1905 and published in 1909.

The Kshatriya usually had roots in the nobility as a warrior, prince, chief, judge or patrician. The kshatriyas could also be monks or householders who were active in uplifting of others.2 The moral values were honor, uprightness and dignity. They respected strength of mind and body while disdaining timidity and weakness. They preferred succinct speech to incessant academic debate and discussion. The character of kshatriyas was marked by the predominance of rajas and sattva; rajas is the principle of activity or energy, while sattva is the principle of purity.3 As was the custom of the Kshatriya, Siddhartha would have been taught the alphabet and numbers at age 3, and by 6 he would have entered a formal educational and a military training program that lasted until age 16.

According to the traditional texts, Siddhartha successfully completed his warrior training and had his graduation ceremony at age 16. The texts say that Siddhartha easily demonstrated his superior martial skills and his father had announced that Siddhartha would become his heir apparent as leader of the clan. Then, according to tradition, he would have been required to further learn and demonstrate his martial prowess with many weapons including the bow, sword, spear, lasso, and battle axe, and Siddhartha would also have had to prove his abilities in fencing, swimming, wrestling, hand-to-hand combat, horsemanship and archery from a moving chariot. Also, often beginning at 6 years old, Kshatriya children would train in Yoga and learn to control their body/mind.

Thus, for a decade, as a young apprentice warrior, Siddhartha would have pursued a rigorous curriculum of studies and military training that required proficiency in all the Indo-Aryan weapons of war, including the chariot, warhorse and elephant. The weapons curriculum was called the dhanurveda (literally "bow knowledge"). The young Kshatriya were taught by experienced warriors. Instruction was personalized, and often students lived in the homes of their instructors for the duration of a course. Sutas or tutors recited to students the Itihasas ("histories") or the achievements of the great warriors and battles of the past. The training emphasized discipline, toughness and endurance. The curriculum also included courses in logic, politics and economics.

The young Kshatriya studied the ancient Vedic religious texts. In life, the Kshatriyas caste members exercised self-discipline in order to serve a God and other sentient beings. Traditionally, the kshatriyas were motivated by dharma, or Right Action. Instead of accumulating material wealth, a kshatriya worked to expand his own skills and identity in order to serve others. According to Paramhansa Yogananda4, they were designated to serve society through their administrative, executive, and protective qualities.

The aptitudes of the ideal kshatriyas were valor, vigor, resourcefulness, fortitude, skill, courage, generosity, and inspirational leadership. They regarded happiness and self-fulfillment as psychological states of mind. For the kshatriyas an inner happiness was based on uplifting the lives of others. Reportedly, a Kshatriya was often very interested in his heritage and had a strong devotion to his people and family and a culture's gods. He enjoyed being physically strong and competing with others. They were considered elite warriors yet noble and righteous. They had a strict moral code to follow; reminiscent of the ideal European medieval Knights and Japanese samurai. There are numerous stories of how a Kshatriya had a strong body and soft heart such as how a warrior cried when he accidentally crushed a flower. Yet, also, they were ruthless in battle. They did not fear death due to a belief in reincarnation.

A Kshatriya was taught and expected to learn very well the martial arts as well as the mastery of his body and mind. He shunned physical softness and accepted a voluntary asceticism in his life of a specific diet, fasting, avoiding intoxicants; training the mind and body to endure hardship. The goal was to find pleasure in the exercise of the will in self-denial. Another goal was not to learn simply abstract knowledge but comprehending knowledge experientially and its useful application. They acted honorably and with restraint to avoid being ensnared and corrupted in the normal world. In sum, the Kshatriya were devoted to fighting valiantly, ruling justly, bringing justice to malefactors, protecting the innocent, keeping order in the land and having a deep loyalty and fidelity to his superiors, his people and his land.

In order to be consecrated as a warrior, a kshatriya was required to demonstrate his competence with weapons. When they passed the test, at the age of sixteen, there was a formal ceremony where he received an official uniform. The consecrated warrior was now allowed to fight in battle, receive the military salute and marry a woman of all Varnas with mutual consent.

Siddhartha, the Kshatriya

As mentioned before, Siddhartha and his family were members of the Kshatriya or warrior/leader caste. Therefore, after clearly demonstrating his warrior skills and being named heir apparent to his father, the nobles of the clan would have been satisfied that he could lead them also in war. Since Siddhartha was not yet Awakened, a reasonable assumption is that he thought and understood the world dualistically and suffered from the ignorance of that perspective. He would have believed in an identity or self, was oriented by his preferences and dislikes through subject /object, he had expectations of others/himself, he experienced anger and greed, craved sense-based pleasures, etc..

The Samyutta texts tells us, "For the kshatriya there is no other rule but to fight," and the Adi Parva that "among men the highest duties are those performed by the kshatriya." Caste sanctions and social conditioning required warriors to be fighters. War was a fundamental reality of the state, and waging it was the primary responsibility of the kshatriya. As a kshatriya as well as heir to the kingdom's leadership, Siddhartha most certainly had an education and training in the caste law, obligation, and duty including protecting the other citizens. This training also in Law and duty is evidenced that the Buddha was often sought for and gave practical advice to Kings and other people.

Ancient legal texts show that it was possible but not encouraged for a warrior to give up the military life and take up a life of asceticism, as Siddhartha did after leaving his father's court at age 29. Even the traditional description of Siddhartha leaving his home shows his warrior class, as he rode his warhorse, carried his broadsword, and his hair, which he cut, was still worn in the warrior's topknot.

Siddhartha's Life Different from the Traditional rendition

Are key elements of the traditionally accepted narrative of Siddhartha's early life reasonable?

First, the prophecy that Siddhartha could be either a great ruler or a great spiritual teacher was culturally accepted at that time. Also, it is understandable that his father Suddhodana preferred, since the kshatriyas were warrior-rulers and Siddhartha was his first born, that his son would continue the family lineage as a ruler of the clan. However, the traditional stories that his father pampered Siddhartha in great luxury and shielded him from knowledge of religion and human suffering as well as keeping him always amused within the family residence are unlikely. After all, the kshatriya rejected an indulgent lifestyle of ease and comfort.

As the eldest son of a noble kshatriya family and the presumptive heir of a chief of a regional power, Siddhartha would have had, as did all males of his caste, rigorous training as a warrior. If he had failed to meet the warrior requirements, Siddhartha would not have successfully graduated his training and he would have been consigned to a life of unimportance. Also, his father wanted him to become a great clan leader, but if Siddhartha had been pampered in great luxury and not have become a tested warrior, he would likely not have been approved by the clan leaders to succeed his father.

Even though Siddhartha's father, Suddhodhana, is usually referred in the texts as a King, it is very unlikely since, at that time, the clans were ruled by a chosen not hereditary leader. The Shakyas' government was organized as a Republican system, not a monarchy; they held regular meetings in which the members of the most influential families took part. It is probably more accurate that Siddhartha's father's status was of a regional leader, as the elected chief of a tribal confederacy - Clan Chief. Lastly, Siddhartha would have known well about death, illness and debilitation (the three sights) because during his life there were frequent wars in his area, and as a warrior he would have been acutely aware of the harmful, even deadly consequences of fighting and war.

Connecting Siddhartha to Buddha

There are other indications in the Buddha's teachings, that he had been thoroughly trained as a kshatriya. For example, the Buddha often used the imagery and vocabulary of a warrior to convey his Dhamma. Words like charioteer, sword and shield, war elephants, banners, fortress, archers, arrows, poisoned arrows, were all clearly used metaphors in expressing the difficult struggle to overcome one's delusions (Mara and its armies). He also emphasized that following the Path of Liberation required similar virtues possessed by warriors. The Buddha's Enlightenment and victory was described as a "battle" between himself and Mara, the embodiment of death and evil.

The suttas frequently describe how the Buddha was often sought out by kings and advisors in governmental and societal matters. As we would expect from his education and training as a Kshatriyas, the texts show that the Buddha had an intimate knowledge of state craft. As a member of the warrior caste and son of a clan leader, the Buddha maintained cordial relations with regional kings and leaders. Numerous suttas in the Pali Canon record his conversations with Kings Pasenadi and Bimbisara and others, showing that the Buddha clearly understood the issues of leaders involved in government. Buddha's doctrine reflected the importance of virtuous state relations and peaceful conflict resolution and coexistence.

The fact that the Buddha was sought out for his wise advice by rulers of kingdoms suggests the high regard in which he and the sangha (the spiritual community composed of four groups: monks, nuns, laymen, and laywomen) were held by the states. Numerous Kingdoms, from the beginning of Buddha's teaching and the Sangha, were important in supporting their sustenance and growth. Even though there are major implications about understanding Siddhartha's personal development through the training and education as a Kshatriyas, in the end, after Awakening the Buddha is quoted, 'One is not called noble who harms living beings. By not harming living beings one is called noble.' His Pacifism is clear. He was now a true spiritual leader and advanced only a personal non-harm ethical life based on compassion and wisdom.

What is the Meaning of Dukkha?

Dukkha was the focus of the Buddha's teachings. "In the past, monks, and also now, I teach Dukkha and the cessation of Dukkha." In order to understand Buddhist doctrine, it is crucial to understand the Dukkha principle, is based on the fact of suffering; its reality, cause, and the means of cessation. While the principle of Dukkha is one of the most important concepts in the Buddhist tradition, its meaning is complex and easily misconstrued. Dukkha in Pāli; (Sanskrit: duhkha) is most often translated as suffering, its philosophical meaning is more complex and is also translated as anxiety, stress, discontent or dissatisfaction. In fact, this concept contains a cluster of interrelated connotations including sorrow, imperfection, unease, anguish and alienation. In Sanskrit, this term is formed from the prefix 'd', which is related to the English 'dis', plus the noun 'kha', which means happiness or with 'ease' meaning freedom from concern, anxiety; a quiet state of mind. The prefix 'dis' gives a word the opposite meaning: perhaps dis-ease, or discontent, agitation or misery could be more concise translations of the Sanskrit term, duhkha, than suffering.

Types of Dukkha

The question which determined Siddhartha's renunciation quest was "What is the cause and cessation of Dukkha?" In analyzing the nature of suffering upon his Awakening, the Buddha explained three basic kinds of Dukkha: 1. Physical and emotional suffering: We are all familiar with these related to: *Body pain *Illness *Debilitation *Injury *Death by accident *Genetically caused disability *pain of disappoint 2. Grief of change: The Dukkha caused by change: *We desire to have what we want and like and once we have it, to keep it, but it doesn't remain, we can't hold onto it. This includes not only physical objects and people but also emotions and experiences. 3. It is a universal malaise or malcontent: a subtle form of Dukkha inherent in all conditioned things and is the most difficult to recognize.

 Deep down, we understand that life is not on 'solid ground' and that our very existence is insecure, constantly transforming and unsubstantial or Anicca. Even our thoughts and mental images as well as our emotions are impermanent. All the mind's constructions, objects or forms are fluctuating and transforming entities. There is also no permanent or substantial self to be found or Anatta - no-self. All identifications, cognitive constructions and overlays are dynamic, ever-changing, complementary and ultimately unsubstantial; grasping, 'having' and attaching to a self or objects or experience or life is inherently unsustainable and ultimately creates dis-ease, discontentment and grief.

Like the familiar idea expresses: If we try to grasp our life experiences like water in our hand, the minute we close our hand and cling tightly to hold on, and keep it, the water seeps through our fingers. While it might be a necessary evolutionary survival mechanism, the illusion of substantiality and permanence foments the unenlightened and ignorant human aspiration to find inherent and everlasting happiness and a self. Therefore, one wrongly believes they can be satisfied and happy when their cravings and most valued aspirations and objects are obtained and held on to – 'frozen' in time and space, so to speak. Also, the unenlightened constantly seek and crave new pleasurable objects, experiences and emotions. They are on a continuous treadmill driving them forward, never stopping but ultimately never reaching a final satisfaction. The unenlightened human perspective mistakenly continuously craves not only to have, but to preserve, accumulate and protect all of one's desired mental/emotional states and possessions including a self, which is inevitably impossible. This creates an existential grief and sorrow.

When conditions in people's lives eventually become precarious, uncertain, unreliable and even catastrophic, they are forced to acknowledge existential insecurities. Then, like Siddhartha with the allegorical first Three sights, they are struck by the fact that life is capricious, groundless and even tragic. Normally, these existential insecurities are ignored or denied, and people live on rationalizations or 'stories' that life is stable, predictable, a universal justice precides and death is still a lifetime away or even never occurs because of an eternal life of a soul. If or when it is realized that these assumptions are fictitious then the accompanying existential crisis with dis-ease or an agitated or frightened and anguished mind and emotions arises.

In his teachings, the Buddha often reminded people that our physical life is finite and uncertain; we can die at any moment; therefore, we shouldn't put off our training for Awakening. There are numerous sections of the suttas emphasizing this point of physical transience and impermanence. For example, in the Siha Sutta (Discourse on the Lion), 'Now, there are gods who are long-lived, beautiful, and very happy, lasting long in their divine palaces. When they hear this teaching by the Realized One (Anicca), they're typically filled with fear, awe, and terror. 'Oh no! It turns out we're impermanent, though we thought we were permanent! It turns out we don't last, though we thought we were everlasting! It turns out we're transient, though we thought we were eternal! It turns out that we're impermanent, not lasting, transient, and included within identity.' And in Sutta Nipata, the Buddha said, *"The world is afflicted by death and decay. But the wise do not grieve, having realized the nature of the world.'* Forms in life are impermanent, uncertain and do not persist.

The Four Sights

In the traditional stories, Siddhartha grew up enjoying many material luxuries and comforts, but at age 29, he had a psychological crisis after seeing the Three Sights of aging, disease, death in the local village; he struggled with the issues of affliction, death, as well as helplessness and debilitation associated with old age.

The story of the Four Sights

This essay proposes that we can best understand these stories as allegorical or representative of the significant impact of three fundamental, existential conditions, common to all living beings, had on the intelligent and thoughtful

Siddhartha. The Four Sights stories are an effective way of conveying the importance of these fundamental existential issues. There are different versions of the story, but all of them share the basic theme. The Four Sights are: aging, disease, death, and hope.

What is the Traditional Four Sights Story?

When Siddhartha was a young man, his father, the 'King', had created a life of opulence and ease for him in the family palace because he did not want Siddhartha to be unhappy and leave, as, at his birth, had been foretold by the holy man could happen. The story goes that despite his father's determination to ensure that he did not encounter any examples of suffering, Siddhartha, when he was 29 years old, was curious about the life outside of the palace, and he asked his attendant to take him around the village just outside the palace walls. Prince Siddhartha ventured out of his palace to the village in a chariot, accompanied by his charioteer Channa. The story continues that Siddhartha first saw a decrepit old man, revealing to him the consequences of aging. When the Prince asked about this person, Channa replied that aging was something that happens to all beings. The second sight was of a person suffering from a debilitating disease. Once again, Siddhartha was shocked at the sight, and Channa explained that all beings are subject to illness and pain. The fact that no one can remain always well and live a pain-free life further troubled the mind of the Prince. The third sight was a rotting corpse of a person who had recently died. As before, Channa explained to the Prince that death is an inevitable fate that happens to everyone. After seeing these three sights, Siddhartha was troubled in his mind and sorrowful about the sufferings that he had seen and that all must endure them in life. Then, Siddhartha came upon the fourth sight; a wandering ascetic who appeared calm and contented. This sight gave the him hope that he too might be released from suffering.

The story continues that the more Siddhartha dwelled upon the Three Sights, the more despair and sorrow he felt about the futility of life. Siddhartha thought: *'What use is my youth and riches and learning, if death will claim it all in the end? Even kings grow old and diseased. Even they surrender to death.'* Here, Siddhartha experienced Samvega. That is a Buddhist term which Bhikkhu Thanissaro defines as: 'The oppressive sense of shock, dismay, and alienation that comes with realizing the futility and meaninglessness of life as it's normally lived; a chastening sense of our own complacency and foolishness in having let ourselves live so blindly; and an anxious sense of urgency in trying to find a way out of the meaningless cycle.'[5]

Aftermath

The story continues that these revelations —old age, disease and death—
shocked and troubled Siddhartha deeply. He kept thinking about the Sights
even though several happy events had been arranged for him upon returning to
the palace. However, Siddhartha wanted to know if there was a possible way to
stop these dreadful three sights. As a result of continuously thinking of the first
three sights, he decided to leave the palace in search of an end to the suffering
of all sentient beings.

Having been inspired by the ascetic, , Siddhartha thought, *'Like that monk, I
must give up trappings that bind me to things that hold no meaning and lead a
simple life. Only then can I bring peace to men.'* He decided to give up
everything and search for the answer to the question, 'What creates people's
suffering and how can it be prevented?' At the age of 29, he left the palace,
accompanied only by Channa. After a short distance, he sent Channa back with
his possessions and continued on, he began an ascetic life, and, at the end of
over six years, he attained Awakening as Gautama Buddha.

While often in the traditional story Siddhartha developed the profound
insights of impermanence and the ultimate dissatisfaction of conditioned
existence immediately after the Four Sights, in fact, they were insights the
Buddha gained through the process of Awakening. In other early Pali suttas,
while the general themes are the same, Siddhartha Gautama's actual going out
of the palace and having the physical encounters with the Sights, are not
mentioned. Rather, Siddhartha's (In)Sights into old age, sickness and death
were portrayed as abstract musings or considerations and psychological
reflections. For example, *'Even though I was endowed with such fortune, such
total refinement, the thought occurred to me: 'When an untaught, run-ofthe-mill
person, himself subject to aging, not beyond aging, sees another who is aged, he
is horrified, humiliated, and disgusted, oblivious to himself that he too is subject
to aging, not beyond aging. If I — who am subject to aging, not beyond aging —
were to be horrified, humiliated, & disgusted on seeing another person who is
aged, that would not be fitting for me.' As I noticed this, the normal young
person's intoxication with my youth entirely dropped away.'*

The reported psychological and emotional crisis of Siddhartha remains the
same whether the story is about his visiting the village or instead only
pondering such themes. However, understanding the full extent and context of
Siddhartha's likely warrior education as a kshatriya, the Four stories are easily
seen as naive and allegorical of his deeper original existential questioning and

concerns. The traditional stories seem too elementary to realistically convey a trained warrior-knight's education, experience and perspective about those existential issues at the age of 29. Therefore, this essay hypothesizes a different perspective about the dilemma that Siddhartha was struggling with, hoping to gain a more insightful perspective as to what caused him to renounce his esteemed clan position and familial responsibilities.

Siddhartha's Existential Crisis

 An insightful perspective of the influences that impacted Siddhartha is available by exploring the important training in the kshatriya caste. By understanding these aspects of Siddhartha's personal story, we will develop an alternative, more realistic profile of his intentions to leave his duties as a future clan leader and become an ascetic seeking Truth.

A consistent profile in the text stories of Siddhartha indicate that he was intelligent and kind and, throughout his life, he had a pacifist nature with empathetic concerns about the well-being of all sentient beings (the texts mention this concern including humans, a swan, snake, birds, worms, and oxen). At a certain life phase, 29 years old and after becoming a father, concerns of life and wellbeing became especially personal for him.

 Siddhartha had a crisis regarding his responsibilities within which the standards of behavior and disposition as a warrior were now unacceptable. So, a new basis of understanding and behavior had to be found at any cost. Siddhartha clearly knew his duty as a kshatriya warrior whose aim included ensuring the rule of the Right and Justice. A significant personal conflict for him was possibly accepting the soon to be responsibilities of the clan ruler's duty- imposed by the creed of the kshatriya warrior- as the only response to the inevitable conflict amongst kingdoms, including war. These traditional rules of war and violence had long been used in response to the hostilities and cruelty of humans versus the use of spiritualized ethics which insists on ahimsa, or non-injuring and non-hostility. As the Buddha later taught; *Hostilities aren't stilled through hostility, regardless. Hostilities are stilled through non-hostility: this, an unending truth.* Dhammapada 5

With the realization, at age 29, that he was soon to become heir as chief of his clan, Siddhartha's warrior/ruler responsibilities would be greatly heightened, and he would be required not only to enforce the rule of his clan but also to lead it against all outside aggressions. He, as the chief of the clan that he loved, as well as the other sentient beings of his kingdom, would become directly entangled in humanities absurd and foolish conflicts and contests which create the inevitability of death, debilitation, great pain and destruction - Dukkha. As the warrior clan leader there was no other acceptable alternative for him except to participate in the endless rounds of violence and Dukkha created through greed and hatred and ignorance. He knew of no exit from his active participation, even leadership, in these countless cycles of violence and suffering.

At this point, as the future clan leader, Siddhartha understood that within the conventional political system, he could not absolve himself from the absurdity and suffering created by the constant conflict, war and death used to resolve problems and gain possessions. So, Siddhartha's inner conscience was clear, he must chose to adopt the inner spiritual ascetic direction; adopting the Path of transcending the violent social duty by the spiritually ethical way of non-harm. His only choice could be pacifism and an opposition to war or violence of any kind with the principle that all conflicts among people and nations should be resolved without recourse to violence or war, this became his conviction. "The Buddha's teaching leads us to the realization that we must always strive to harm no sentient being, human or nonhuman, whether or not it is in our selfish interest to do so."6

To pursue this conviction and to find an effective resolution to his personal crisis, Siddhartha had to shun the expected obligations as a warrior/ruler and the world driven by all its selfish aims and actions justified with ignorance. In the end, after leaving his residence and clan lands, and six years of intense spiritual training, Siddhartha became Awakened and the Buddha. After finding the ultimate resolution to his existential dilemma- Dukkha and its origin, and cessation- and through teaching his dharma, Buddha returned to the Knight's creed of uplifting others, while also recognizing ahimsa or non-harm as the highest spiritual-ethical Truth. As Chatsumarn Kabilsingh wrote, *The first precept in Buddhism is "Do not kill." This precept is not merely a legalistic prohibition, but a realization of our affinity with all who share the gift of life. A compassionate heart provides a firm ground for this precept.'*

The Buddha also established the Sangha when he recognized the value for ascetic renunciation as an effective way to the solution of ignorance. As the Buddha, he asserted the compatibility between human action and a spiritual life lived in union with the highest states of wisdom, compassion and consciousness.

A Psychological Explanation of Existential Crisis/Depression

This section will briefly discuss the definition of existential crisis and its comparison to the descriptions of Siddhartha's psychological and emotional response to his crisis of clearly, deeply and personally comprehending the allegorical three sights.

An existential crisis occurs when an individual questions their life's meaning, purpose, or value. It is often expressed with depression and anxiety or negative speculations. It focuses on the purpose in life, like when a person questions, 'What is my greater purpose? How should I live my life?' Existential depression may occur when a person comes face to face with issues of life, death, freedom and the meaning of life. Existential depression may be characterized by a unique sense of hopelessness that our lives may have no essence. For instance, several other existential questions can be asked such as; 'What is the meaning of life? = What is the meaning (essence) of existence?, What is my true nature/essence?, What is my true identity?, Is there a god that cares about us? If so, why do innocent and good people die early and without meaning?"

There is also a premise that existential depression is a form of a spiritual crisis when someone questions and intensely examines their overall belief system, or what existence in life is for. In summary, they may question life's very purpose and the meaning of existence. Existential psychiatrist Irvin Yalom believes an existential crisis can center on a person's concern and attempts to make sense of four main topics: death, isolation, freedom, and meaninglessness. It can be experienced at different life stages.

 A theory developed by psychologist and psychiatrist Kazimierz Dabrowski states that existential depression can be a positive catalyst for change and growth. That it forms part of the process of 'positive disintegration'. His idea is that people, especially gifted and creative people, learn and grow in a positive way from their traumatic experiences and life crises. Siddhartha experienced his crisis perhaps phrased as such; *'What creates the constant discontentment and craving that pushes leaders and common people to never be happy or satisfied but instead become angry, greedy, brutal, cruel and even cause wars?'* He felt Saṃvega, the sense of shock, anxiety and spiritual urgency to find liberation and find an escape and the cessation of the causes of life's absurdities that are mostly created by the actions of human beings. As he later described in a sermon (The Fire Sermon) *'The world of the senses and mental formations are 'burning" with passion, aversion, delusion and suffering'.*

Siddhartha's experience of alienation and angst is very similar to what psychology now calls an Existential Crisis. In the case of Siddhartha, his questioning and dilemma hypothetically could have been; '*When I become the clan leader/warrior, I must lead and fight wars in which my family, my son, friends, my clan will suffer and probably die. Why must this be so? Why does this sufferance which creates wars and cruelty exist? This suffering of wars and cruelties of humans is created by the consequences of the human mind not gods. I need to find the answer to what the root causes of this suffering are, so I can stop it.*'

He knew so very well from the heroic stories told in his childhood by his tutors, that the misery created by humans especially in wars and battles are the norm in history; and this curse would continue. So Siddhartha was striving to respond to his deep training and perspective as a kshatriya warrior/knight whose sworn duty was justice, to govern virtuously, extend peace and happiness to all subjects, protecting the innocent, keeping order in the land, a 'defender of the poor' and counsel in matters of ethical dilemmas, from the depth of his conscience and emotions he perhaps pleaded, *How can I stop it!*

There is also existential anxiety that includes feelings of panic, agitation, or dread about the nature of an individual's or human existence. Any related perplexity such as "What am I doing with my life? may result in a panic attack or other symptoms of anxiety. Someone in existential crisis may experience existential aloneness; the feeling that there is no one else who can relate to how they feel in their lives. At the point of absolute crisis, Siddhartha realized that he had no one to turn to for answers…only himself. He, alone, had to choose. He choose to leave his family, clan and role of leader to seek a resolution to his seemingly impenetrable dilemma. Leaving was his resolution; his quest'and his answer came after six intense years of introspective study of the spiritual conduits of his time.

The Responses of Siddhartha's Crisis

It is proposed here that the descriptions of the thoughts and behaviors of Siddhartha in the Aftermath, his Samvega, are more convincing as descriptions of his real renunciation crisis than the traditional story of his feeling angry and betrayed by the King, his father, for hiding the Three sights from him as he grew up.

The Responses of Siddhartha's Crisis showing Anxiety and Depression:

- Rumination: After observing the Sights the prince was very upset and he kept on dwelling unhappily about the suffering in the sights for a long time.

- Symptoms of depression: After seeing the Three sights, Siddhartha was troubled in his mind and sorrowful about the sufferings that he and others must endure in life. For example, he lost interest in previous pleasurable social activities and he felt agitated and restless.

- Re-evaluation of life values and goals caused by depressive reaction: According to the sutta Siddhartha thought: *'Even though I was endowed with such fortune, such total refinement, the thought occurred to me: 'When an untaught, run-of-the-mill person, himself subject to aging, not beyond aging, sees another who is aged, he is horrified, humiliated, and disgusted, oblivious to himself that he too is subject to aging, not beyond aging. If I — who am subject to aging, not beyond aging — were to be horrified, humiliated, and disgusted on seeing another person who is aged, that would not be fitting for me.' As I noticed this, the typical young person's intoxication with youth entirely dropped away.'*

- Re-evaluation: according to the sutta Siddhartha thought: *'And what is ignoble search? There is the case where a person, being subject himself to birth, seeks happiness in what is likewise subject to birth. Being subject himself to aging... illness... death... sorrow... defilement, he seeks happiness in what is likewise subject to illness... death... sorrow... defilement.'*

- Reaction to situation with Depression: He felt helplessness and hopelessness. He developed a bleak outlook— that nothing will ever get better and there's nothing he could do to escape the situation of the inevitability of the Dukkha in life. He could not accept the fact that humans would suffer so much.

- Questioning of previous Faith, Beliefs and Revaluation: in fact, these incidents made him reflect on life deeply and he did not accept the fact that people are born to suffer in life like in a tragedy. A life destined to fear, conflict, war, famine and debilitation- what is the sense! He returned to the palace troubled and obsessed with this existential dilemma. Human suffering had a great impact on Siddhartha. Perhaps there was a way out of the suffering and the holy life would show him.

He became aroused to the idea that the futility in living a life of materialism, greed, revenge, hatred, egotism is best given up in favor of the spiritual life of finding the answer to this horrible inheritance of all living creatures, and so he wanted desperately to begin an ascetic life.

- Radical life change motivation: His drastic motivation to leave the palace, his family and the responsibilities of being a warrior prince and future clan leader because, he sought a creative solution for the higher dilemma which had to do with the cause of humans suffering in life. After over six years of investigating and following the ascetic life with important gurus of his time, it was through his genius and innovation that he creatively discovered the radical solution to the dilemma and the cessation of Dukkha- Awakening - Nibbana.

- The Ending of the Crisis through Awakening: There are wars, famine, accidents causing debilitating injury and death, personal abuse, as well as illness, and many are maladies that always accompany life. As a kshatriya knight, Siddhartha saw that people are surrounded by these as well as greed, hatred and senseless aggression, anger, hostility and crime. He reflected that as it is now, in all these things, there is nothing one can apparently do to remain secure, and, therefore, life is not only perplexing but existentially insecure and anxious ridden.

The Awakening of Siddhartha

Siddhartha felt overwhelmed by the Dukkha of the never-ending manifestation of debilitation and death and illness, consequently, he had an existential crisis. Yet he wanted to protect his clan, family, sentient beings and other humans from the seemingly endless folly of human ignorance that creates Dukkha. He chose renunciation to resolve this perplexity. So, it was during Siddhartha's six years of ethical and bhavana or contemplation and spiritual cultivation, he became Awakened and as the Buddha or Awakened One, he discovered three universal characteristics of life: Impermanence, No Self and Interconnectedness of all life, or Dependent Origination. And from these insights he proclaimed the Four Noble Truths: There is Dukkha; There is a cause of Dukkha; There is a cessation to Dukkha; and there is a Way- The Eightfold Path for the cessation.

Out of compassion for all sentient beings, Buddha formulated the teachings of the Noble Eightfold Path in a way that other people could achieve Awakening. Then he began his duty of teaching to enlighten the world and the cessation of

Dukkha. In fact, while the Buddha identified himself as an Awakened human being, he never claimed any divinity. He had begun his spiritual search created by his existential crisis of his abhorrence of the continual discontent, unhappiness and cruelty of humans that created never ending generational cycles of suffering.

Of all the creatures that exist on this earth, only a human can ask the questions that the Buddha did and alter their behaviors and kamma or intentions as well. The nature of Siddhartha's questions, emotions, search and dilemma has been and is still shared by other sensitive, intelligent and questioning humans. Therefore, Siddhartha's legendary life showing his reactions, pain and aspirations are important because they reflect a universal question -How is human discontent, unhappiness and suffering created and what is the cure? Questions which have been asked throughout history by many thoughtful, perplexed and sorrowful people. This existential ignorance creates anxiety, agitation, a malaise, discontentment, unhappiness, disillusionment and alienation, not only psychologically, but it is also expressed through action, words and deeds.

Siddhartha's crisis perhaps began with asking, 'What is the cause of this continual pestilence, war, famine, and death, that can destroy clans, families, cities and the dear creatures of this earth? How can life be so arbitrary and heartless? What anguished Siddhartha was not knowing the underlying cause of the suffering of all sentient beings. He knew of the obvious consequences of greed, hatred, malcontent, and cruelty that were very clear to him especially through his training as warrior-knight devoted to the protection of the people of his realm from all harm.

This question troubled Siddhartha greatly and being at the age of transition into fatherhood as well as soon becoming the leader of his clan, for this young, healthy, vibrant and sensitive person, this existential condition of life became an obsession. He became depressed, his vibrancy became low as Siddhartha thought that his life, as well as the life of his family, other humans and all the animals who wanted to live happily, were, under the present conditions of ignorance, inevitably going to be filled with misery and there was nothing he could to prevent it. As the Buddha said: "*All beings tremble before violence. All love life. All fear death. See yourself in others. Then whom can you hurt? What harm can you do?*" This was perhaps the existential crisis that he faced in the traditional story of the Four Sights. Therefore, very likely, he hoped to find the deeper, new answer of the cause and prevention of this dukkha from happening to his family and clan- to everyone.

The anxious sense of urgency for him was to leave the palace in order to try to find a cessation of the horror and to resolve this existential dilemma. In the end, this questioning of this existential condition of our existence is given an answer by the Buddha that is unique and does not fly into the suppositions of supernaturalism and divine forces that, in fact, the Buddha did not believe are involved directly in the existence of creatures on this earth.

The Buddha saw the continual metaphysical and philosophical debates about certain questions as not only unfruitful but as a distraction. For example, in the CulaMalunkyovada Sutta (The Unanswered Questions) Ven. Malunkyaputta asked the Buddha four primary questions, one being, *"Is the world eternal, or not?"* and the Buddha would not answer this and the other questions. Why? Because the questions were (hence any answer would be to) dualistic. They relate to common relative reality which creates clinging to the ignorance of believing duality - a root of our dukkha. Answering would reinforce dualism: me-you, space-time, object and subject. So, the Buddha left his answers "undeclared" since they are unfruitful to the spiritual practice, and they might set-back one's practice with cognitive constructions of duality. Therefore, he did not participate in those discussions that were and still are so common for the human mind to enjoy the speculation and identification of different possible scenarios.

Scholars assert that throughout history this existential dilemma was not only the preoccupation of Siddhartha, but religions have been founded on finding a solution by asserting divine intervention in rewarding good vs bad behaviors as well as for the desired continuation of self with a belief in the soul and personalized God and eternal life. Philosophers have also questioned this endlessly. Scientists have written extensively on the question of 'What is life?' in trying to find a scientific perspective of understanding the reason of our existence, on this planet, within this immense and timeless universe. Yet, Siddhartha's quest and Awakening which cogently answered this existential dilemma of Dukkha has been, for over 2500 years, and continues today and into the future, the foundation, the Path and deliverance from ignorance for millions of people.

Conclusions

Siddhartha's crisis and quest (resulting in his Awakening) has been one that humanity has shared for eons: the malaise of agonizing over why do humans act in such cruel and horrible ways to each other and all other sentient beings, and with all the accompanying psychological suffering and grief; how can this suffering be attenuated?

Remedies to the Existensial Crisis

Most people try different remedies to this crisis:

• Ignoring by making drastic changes with hedonistic acting out, to bring more distraction with sensual intensity into one's life, like bringing back the excitement of youth, buying fancy cars, getting an 'exciting' new job, or acting as in the phrase to 'Burn the candle at both ends'.

• Continuing to suffer but accepting the apparent meaninglessness of life and living with that acceptance of muddling through a baffling and distressing life.

• Taking up a faith, metaphysically dualistic based religion which promises a heavenly existence and union with the divine upon death. Rejecting rationality and giving blind faith to a certain set of beliefs, which gives one denial and hope while covering up the despair, the fear, dissatisfaction.

• Finding the answers that the Buddha discovered; the key to unlocking the answer to an existentially meaningful and content life. However, as the Buddha realized after his Awakening: *'This truth which I have realized is profound, difficult to see, abstruse, calming, subtle, and not attainable through mere sophisticated logic. But beings revel in attachment, take pleasure in attachment and delight in attachment. For beings who thus revel, take pleasure and delight in attachment, this is an extremely difficult thing to see: that is, the law of conditionality, the principle of Dependent Origination. Moreover, this also is an extremely difficult thing to see: the calming of all conditioning, the casting off of all clinging... cessation, Nibbāna.'* It is an insightful truth that takes time and effort to ripen to fruition. Buddha discovered the answer, not in the common dualistic framework, but in the non-dualistic, transcendent Awakening, where separation and alienation are no longer possible.

This interconnectedness is all embracing. As I relate in my book, The Buddha's Radical Psychology: Explorations, 2017, to see the connectedness of all things is to see that not a thing has an independent existence, and that our 'world' or loka, is cognitively created or only mental fabrications. In other words, he became aware that the structuring of our world is dependent on our cognitive processes and abstract categories of sensation are constructed by the way we perceive, name, categorize, and differentiate them. *'All experiences are preceded by mind, having mind as their master, created by mind.'* Buddha

Our 'world', as well as our 'I', is subjectively constructed and if believed to be inherently substantial are indeed 'Illusions'. In addition, the Buddha's Enlightenment was a life-altering experience which gave him a radically new perspective. Awakening, or pure experience, unveiled for the Buddha the cognitively-based, dependent, complementary relationship of the subject-object world. In other words, his Awakened mind became liberated of the dichotomy of subject and object. This was a crucial distinction between mind and mind events. Dukkha, as existential malaise, was transcended and was no longer possible because he understood it is a manifestation of ignorance created through the dualism of subject/object, identification and separation.

With Awakening; the Dukkha of disillusionment, craving, greed, discontentment, selfishness, alienation, anxiety about death and conflict, even war, come to an end. Once the perspective of nondualism was achieved, this was the end of Siddhartha's search to answer the dilemma of existential insecurity and sorrow: *'Oh housebuilder! You are seen, you shall build no house (for me) again. All your rafters are broken, your roof-tree is destroyed. My mind has reached the unconditioned (Nibbana); the end of craving has been attained.* Buddha (Commentary: The rafters of this self-created house (rebirth) are defilements. The ridgepole is ignorance, the root of all defilements. The shattering of the ridgepole of ignorance by wisdom results the end of construction (rebirth). With the demolition the house, the Mind attains the Unconditioned, which is Nirvana.)

The Buddha's Awakening was achieved by Bhavana or meditation and virtuous, ethical behavior, through the gradual development and cultivation and purification of his mind, of letting go of the layered cognitive constructions until finally he realized the point of seeing without the Illusion created by the cognition veil of dualistic constructions. The question of existential angst was answered in the sense that it doesn't exist except in the realm of our cognitive ignorance. This was his liberation, and this is what he taught. Through the Buddha's meditative and ethical Path, our world of cognitive constructions become understood. In incremental stages, there is a dissolving of the 'normal' conceptual categories which leads to a clarity of one's state of mind to 'see things as they are' and the end of dukkha.

Through a systematic Bhavana practice, we can free our perceptions from all the restraints and burdens of the preenlightened mind and achieve Awakening – 'Emptiness'. Through his meditation experience, the Buddha came to understand that his experiential objective 'world' was interdependent with his subjectivity and that the systematic cognitive organization is the matrix. So Awakening consists in seeing and reflecting on things just as they are, impartially, without exclusion, bias, attachment, obstructions, or distortion. The grasper-grasped relationship ceases. Craving ends, the 'flame' of craving is extinquished.

With Awakening, one experiences the Bliss of the Buddha and lives life with well-being, compassion and wisdom while still appreciating the mysterious, veiled nature of existence.

Summary

In summary, this paper proposes that Siddhartha, understood at a crucial time of his life that, as the future clan ruler, he would be trapped and obligated to fully participate in the assumptions, rules, systems and actions causing suffering created by ignorance. If he joined that cultural and political system out of caste duty and obligation, he would be involved in the continual perpetuation of violence and suffering created by the malcontent cravings of humans living with and in ignorance. As the Clan Warrior chief, he would have been a purveyor of the suffering, absurdity, foolishness and the unwholesomeness of greed and hatred flamed by arrogance and ignorance.

Finally, through his deep conscience, his intuitive 'Original Mind', together with his inherent sensitivity, kindness and compassion for all sentient beings, this earnest young man, accepted the ethical rule of Asthma or non- harm and asserted his Pacifism. Thereby, Siddhartha relinquished a secular life of vanity, power and glory. Along with his signature pacifism and rejection of war, as the Buddha, he discarded the very notion that the warrior class possessed any moral legitimacy as seen in this quote, *'Though one may conquer a thousand times a thousand men in battle, yet he indeed is the noblest victor who conquers himself.'* Dhammapda 103

Upon leaving his family and clan in renunciation, Siddhartha earnestly struggled to resolve some basic existential questions about life and humanity's existence and conditions which create suffering. After six years of strict asceticism, he realized that none of the practices had provided him with the answer to his question, so he took food and water and bathed in a river to regain his health. He sat under the Bodhi Tree, entered a deep contemplative Jhana state, and gained insight into the extent to which our total world of experience is dependent on a cognitive apparatus which we use to make 'sense' of, or construct, our experience. Abstract categories of sensation are constructed by the way we perceive, name, categorize, and differentiate them. Our 'world', as well as our 'I', is subjectively constructed by our cognitive apparatus or often referred to as 'Mind'. He discovered the three universal truths of Impermanence, Interrelatedness or Dependent Origination and No-self.

The Buddha's Awakening allowed him to discover the answer to the question of suffering and was the culmination of the Buddha's long spiritual journey. Pure experience, unveiled for the Buddha the cognitively-based, dependent, complementary relationship of the subject-object dualistic world. In other words, his enlightened mind became free of the dichotomy of the dualism of subject and object. This was a crucial distinction between mind and mind events. 'Mind' is understood as a direct awareness without any conceptualization, while mind events arise immediately when they become identified with an object. So, although there is a mind at pure experience that exists without mental events, it is not normally experienced. It was through this experience of Emptiness that the Buddha experiencedOneness. This pure experience was a psychological transformation; it created a state of freedom for the Buddha – a realization that all things are empty or unsubstantial – which led him to the cessation of craving, identification, and Dukkha.

The meditation process that led to the achievement of Enlightenment was incremental during which the Buddha gained insights into the incompatibility of his multiple cognitive constructions with the possibility of seeing without illusion. Awakening is achieved only through a gradual process of psychological transformation – his was the Eight-factor Path. But only the Buddha could point out that one cannot win release from form by resorting to the formless. Release from both should be the aim. How could that come about? By the cessation of the consciousness that discriminates between form and formlessness.

The aim of all Buddhist training is understanding the Transcendental Reality with which egotistic intention and craving is released and freeing oneself from ignorance. Pre-enlightened individuals do not know what this is, but they often have an intuition of something different. Reality's true nature is hidden from us by the veils of ignorance. The state of enlightenment is called Nibbāna, and it is inherently selfless (anatta). It is beyond the realm of duality, which is that of subject and object, or self and other-than-self. In Awakening and experiencing the truth of a phenomenon called shunyata, or Emptiness, Siddhartha now as the Buddha answered his original existential question about the cause of Dukkha. As the Buddha, he understood that phenomenon does not possess an inherent, substantial essence or nature. When a person or subject sees something dualistically, the object seen is interpreted as something permanent.

In other words, once the illusion of duality is discovered – there is no one to see and nothing to see; there is only a seeing. One becomes disenchanted and disillusioned just as the person seeing through the illusion of a magic trick, and after that he or she does not take it seriously. With emptiness, the Buddha found that things do not truly exist as we mistakenly believe they do, and that they are empty of a falsely imputed inherent solitary existence. Ultimately, it is because the unenlightened believe their confused projections (ignorance) that they suffer and experience craving, greed, and hatred. The Buddha taught the Dhamma as a remedy to the ignorance and hence Dukkha.

In conclusion, correct cognition is defined as the removal of the obstacles that prevent us from seeing dependent causal conditions in the way they actually arise. These causal foundations are cognitive, not metaphysical; they are the mental and perceptual conditions by which sensations and thoughts occur. What is known through enlightened cognition is 'how things are'. Enlightened cognition is defined as free of all cognitive errors. As Luang Pu Doon, the late master of the forest tradition from Surin, Thailand said: *'In fact the arahants ... fully understand dependent origination. They cease searching; they cease having fabricating mental activities. This is all there is to it. And it all ends here. What remains is only pure, clean, bright, empty. It is Great Emptiness'*. 8 The Buddha was ultimately able to elucidate cogent, powerful and significant doctrines about a transcendent and insightful understanding of our experience of living. It is through the Right Understanding of his doctrines that people are set free from the world of Dukkha and there is the possibility of a world dominated by compassion, empathy and wisdom.

Bibliography

1. Jaspal R. (2011). Caste, social stigma and identity processes. Psychol. Dev. Soc. 23 27–62.

2. Chung, T. (2015). Himalaya Calling: The Origins Of China And India. World Scientific.

3. Yogananda, P. (2003). Autobiography of a Yogi. Chapter 41, "An Idyl in South India." Sterling Publishers Pvt. Ltd.

4. Kriyananda, S., & Yogananda (Paramahansa). (2007). The essence of the bhagavad gita. Chapter 31. Crystal Clarity Publishers.

5. Bhikkhu T. Affirming the Truths of the Heart: The Buddhist Teachings on Samvega & Pasada. Access to Insight, 8 March 2011, http://www.accesstoinsight.org/lib/authors/thanissaro/affirmin g.html. Retrieved on 30 July 2013.

6. Phelps, N. (2004). The great compassion: Buddhism and animal rights. Lantern Books.

7. Kotler, A. (Ed.). (1999). Engaged Buddhist reader: Ten years of engaged Buddhist publishing. Parallax Press. Or: Sahn, S. (1997). The compass of Zen. Shambhala Publications.

8. Ṭhānissaro, B. (2016). Gifts He Left Behind: The Dhamma Legacy of Phra Ajaan Dune Atulo. Access to Insight, 16 June 2011.

9. Books by Rodger R Ricketts, Psy.D.; The Buddha's Teaching: Seeing Without Illusion, Rev.Ed. (2020), The Buddha's Radical Psychology: Explorations (2020) and The Buddha's Gift: A life of Well Being and Wisdom. (2017)